BENDY

RIGBY
INTERACTIVE LIBRARY

© 1996 Rigby Education
Published by Rigby Interactive Library,
an imprint of Rigby Education,
division of Reed Elsevier, Inc.
500 Coventry Lane,
Crystal Lake, IL 60014

Cover designed by Herman Adler Design Group
Designed by Heinemann Publishers (Oxford) Ltd
Illustrations by Samantha Elmhurst
Printed in China

00 99 98 97 96
10 9 8 7 6 5 4 3 2 1

Library of Congress Cataloging-in-Publication Data

Warbrick, Sarah, 1964-
What is bendy?/Sarah Warbrick.
   p.   cm. -- (What is--?)
Summary: Illustrates that many common things found in everyday life
have the physical quality of being able to bend.
ISBN 1-57572-049-3 (library)
1. Matter--Properties--Juvenile literature. 2. Bending--Juvenile literature. [1.Bending. 2. Matter--Properties.]
 I. Title. II. Series: Warbrick, Sarah, 1964- What is--?
QC173.36.W36 1996
620.1'1244--dc20

95-41118
CIP
AC

Acknowledgments
The publishers would like to thank the following for the kind
loan of equipment and materials used in this book:
Early Learning, Bishop Stortford. Toys Я Us Ltd,
the world's biggest toy megastore.

Special thanks to Bryan, George, Jodie, Joel, and Michael
who appear in the photographs

Photographs: Action Plus pp14–15; Bruce Coleman p8;
S&O Matthews pp18, 19; TSW p10; other photographs by Trevor Clifford
Commissioned photography arranged by Hilary Fletcher

There are bendy things all around us.
Bendy things can be fun.
Bendy things can be useful.
But be careful—if things bend too far,
they can break!

This book shows you what is bendy.

These things look different.
What differences can you see?

In one way they are the same.
They are all bendy.

This train is made of
cars linked together.

It bends around the track.

This bridge is made from
lots of pieces of wood.

Look how it bends when you
stand on it.

The cat's tail is bendy.

This is a skeleton of a cat's tail.
Look at the small bones, linked together.

How can this ballet dancer bend so far backward?

The bones in her back are linked to
help her bend.

Look at all this licorice.

It is very bendy.
Brian can make all sorts of
different shapes.

The pole vaulter is using a long pole to help him jump very high.

The pole bends as he flies into the air.

Look at these tent poles.
They look strong and straight.

But they bend easily to
help Michael put up the tent.

Do you think this metal bar can bend?

If it is heated, it will bend.

What is bendy here?

DATE DUE

JUN 0 1 2000	
JUN 2 7 2000	
AUG 0 9 2000	
SEP 1 3 2000	
JAN 3 1 2001	
AUG 0 9 2002	